the art of IMPROVISATION

Rich Matteson
Jack Petersen

An approach to jazz improvisation for the beginning player. The rhythm section is recorded on the left channel with the melodies and solos on the right channel. By lowering the right channel of your stereo player you remove the recorded solos enabling you to play along with the rhythm section.

MMO

7006

For use by all instruments.
Complete C, Bb, Eb and Bass Clef music enclosed.

vol. 2

TABLE OF CONTENTS

WE SINCERELY HOPE THAT THIS RECORDING WILL AID YOU IN YOUR GROWTH AS A JAZZ IMPROVISER. PRACTICE WITH IT EVERY DAY, ALWAYS CONCENTRATING.

BE HONEST WITH YOURSELF AND DO NOT ALLOW MISTAKES TO GO UNCORRECTED. EVERYONE MAKES MISTAKES WHILE TRYING TO CREATE NEW IDEAS. DO NOT LET THESE MISTAKES INTIMIDATE YOU OR KEEP YOU FROM TRYING AGAIN AND AGAIN.

NO ONE WAS BORN KNOWING HOW TO PLAY JAZZ – EVEN THE GREATEST JAZZ MUSICIANS HAD TO DEVELOP AND PERFECT THEIR MUSICAL TALENT THROUGH HONEST, HARD WORK. YOU MUST DO THE SAME.

HAVE FUN WITH YOUR MUSIC, FOR MUSIC EXISTS TO GIVE PLEASURE TO THE PERFORMER AND THE LISTENER.

GOOD LUCK!!

Rich Matteson

This record is Volume II in a series of MMO lp's designed to help teachers and students develop improvisational techniques. It is suggested that the student study Volume I before progressing to Volume II.

The entire volume is based on the Mixolydian mode; all chords used are dominant 7th chords. Because each chord must be treated as a V 7 chord comprising the first, third, fifth and seventh degrees of the Mixolydian mode, each will use its own Mixolydian scale.

The charts below will help you understand the Mixolydian mode and how it can be used with the dominant 7th (V 7) chord.

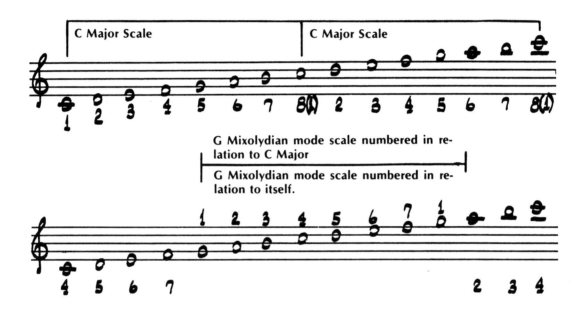

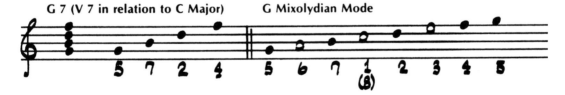

All the notes listed above are numbered to show their relationship to C Major.

All the notes below are numbered to show their relationship to G Mixolydian mode.

682

TUNING GUIDE

Instruments in C

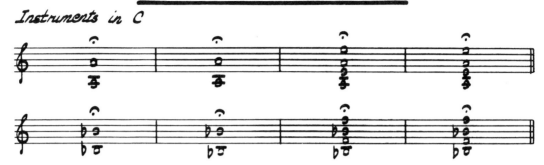

Exercise I

This tune was composed using the 1st, 2nd, 3rd, and 4th notes (degrees) of the G Mixolydian mode. After playing the melody, you should improvise by using all the notes in the mode. (At this stage of your development, do not use any other notes.)

The notes of the G Mixolydian mode are:

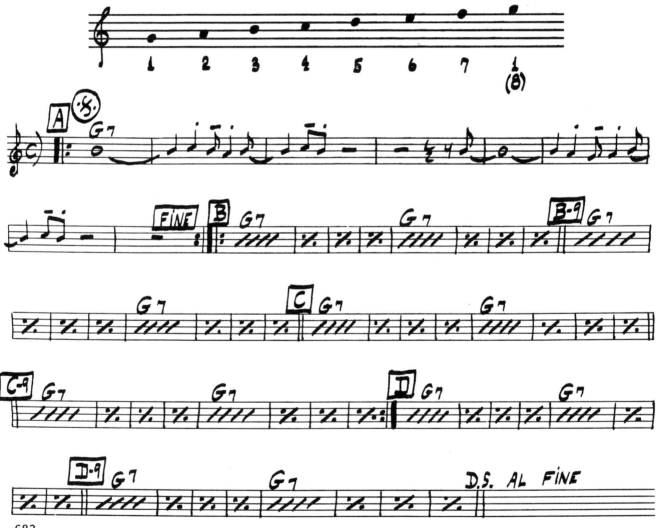

682

6

Exercise 2

This tune uses only the 1st, 5th, and 7th notes (degrees) of the Bb Mixolydian mode. After playing the melody, improvise using all of the notes in the mode.

The notes of the Bb Mixolydian mode are:

Exercise 3

This tune was composed by putting Exercises 1 and 2 together. It is 24 bars long. Each chorus is constructed by the following chord progression:

G 7th for 8 bars. (G Mixolydian mode.)
Bb 7th for 8 bars. (Bb Mixolydian mode.)
G 7th for 8 bars. (G Mixolydian mode.)

Make sure you change correctly from one Mixolydian mode to the other as indicated by the chord changes. Notice that there are four notes which appear in both the G Mixolydian and the Bb Mixolydian modes. They are: G, C, D, and F. Use these notes as pivot notes in your improvisation when changing from one mode to the other.

682

Exercise 4

This tune was composed by using the 1st, 3rd, 5th, 6th, and 7th, notes (degrees) in the C Mixolydian mode. After playing the melody, you should improvise by using all the notes in the mode.

The notes of the C Mixolydian mode are:

682

Exercise 5

This tune uses the 1st, 2nd, 5th and 6th notes (degrees) in the F Mixolydian mode. After playing the melody, try improvising, using all the notes in the mode.

The notes of the F Mixolydian mode are:

Exercise 6

This tune was composed combining Exercises 4 and 5. It is 24 bars long. Each chorus is constructed on the following chord progression:

C 7th for 8 bars. (C Mixolydian mode.)
F 7th for 8 bars. (F Mixolydian mode.)
C 7th for 8 bars. (C Mixolydian mode.)

As in exercise 3, make sure you change correctly from one Mixolydian mode to the other as indicated by the chord changes. Again, there are six notes held in common by both the C and the F Mixolydian modes. They are C, D, F, G, A and Bb. These notes may be used as pivot notes for changing from one mode to the other, as you improvise.

682

Matteson Avenue

This tune is 16 bars long, and is based on two chords: G7 and C7. You will be using the G Mixolydian mode and the C Mixolydian mode. The six common tones between these modes are: G, A, C, D, E, and F.

Bad Day At Jack Rock

This tune is 12 bars long. It is in rock style and based on three chords: G 7, Bb 7, and C 7. You will be using the G Mixolydian, Bb Mixolydian, and C Mixolydian, modes. There are four notes which appear in all three of these modes. They are: G, C, D, And F. Use those common tones as pivot notes when changing from one chord to another.

Twelve Bars of Greens

This tune is twelve bars long, followed by repeats. It is based on three chords: F 7, Bb 7, C 7. You will be using the F Mixolydian, the Bb Mixolydian, and the C Mixolydian, modes. There are five notes held in common among these three. They are: F, G, Bb, C, and D.

12 Bars of Greens (Slow Version)

When playing this version, do not take the first ending after letter F. Take the second ending and D.S. al Fine.

Cycle Song

'Cycle Song' is eight measures long, and then repeats. It is based on four chords, with chord changes every two measures. The four chords are: G 7, C 7, F 7, and Bb 7. You will use the G Mixolydian mode, the C Mixolydian mode, the F Mixolydian mode and the Bb Mixolydian mode. There are four notes that appear in all of these modes. These are: G, C, D, and F. You will find still more common tones appearing between the chords as you play this tune. For example,

There are six common tones in the G and C Mixolydian modes. There are also six common tones in the C and F Mixolydian modes. There are six common tones in the F and Bb Mixolydian modes, and four in the Bb and G Mixolydian modes. See if you can find them, and use them to create musical patterns that will fit both chords. When you listen to the soloists on the record, you will hear them do this. You will also hear them playing notes that are outside the mode.

These are passing tones, and they may be used, but only with care. If you play a note that is not in the Mixolydian mode of a chord, you should then resolve that note by moving into a note that *is* in the mode. For example, if you are improvising to a G 7, using the G Mixolydian mode, and you play an A-flat, you should then play a note, such as an A-natural or a G, that is in the G Mixolydian mode. These "non-chordal" notes will add much to your melodic motion, as they help to build and release tension. However, do not use them in a careless manner, or your improvising will sound unorganized. Creating a good jazz solo is like creating a good recipe: Don't use more sugar than necessary, but don't use too much vinegar, either!!!

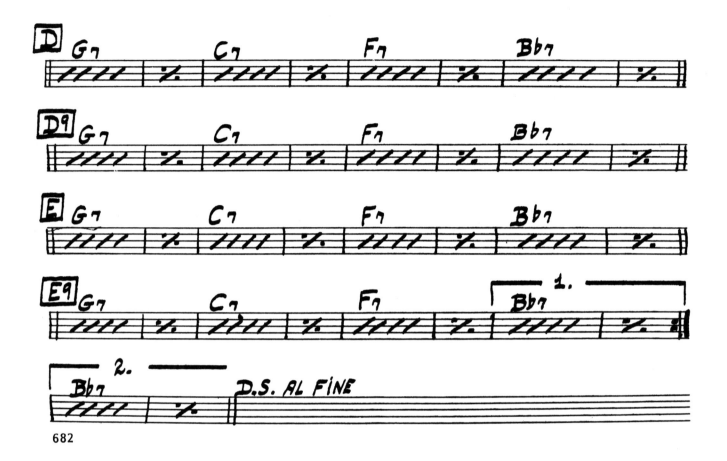

682

After working with Volume I and Volume II, you will find that Volumes III and IV are the next logical steps for you to take in your approach to jazz improvisational studies. Practice seriously and diligently, and we wish you pleasure and good luck!

—Rich Matteson

This record is Volume II in a series of MMO lp's designed to help teachers and students develop improvisational techniques. It is suggested that the student study Volume I before progressing to Volume II.

The entire volume is based on the Mixolydian mode; all chords used are dominant 7th chords. Because each chord must be treated as a V 7 chord comprising the first, third, fifth and seventh degrees of the Mixolydian mode, each will use its own Mixolydian scale.

The charts below will help you understand the Mixolydian mode and how it can be used with the dominant 7th (V 7) chord.

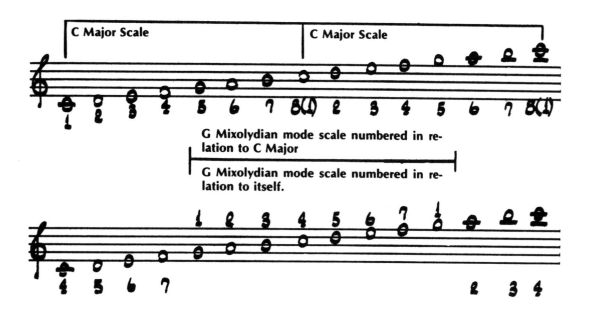

All the notes listed above are numbered to show their relationship to C Major.

All the notes below are numbered to show their relationship to G Mixolydian mode.

TUNING GUIDE

Exercise I

This tune was composed using the 1st, 2nd, 3rd, and 4th notes (degrees) of the A Mixolydian mode. After playing the melody, you should improvise by using all the notes in the mode. (At this stage of your development, do not use any other notes.)

The notes of the A Mixolydian mode are:

682

Exercise 2

This tune uses only the 1st, 5th, and 7th notes (degrees) of the C Mixolydian mode. After playing the melody, you should improvise by using all of the notes in the mode.

The notes of the C Mixolydian mode are:

Exercise 3

This tune was composed by putting Exercises 1 and 2 together. It is 24 bars long. Each chorus is constructed by the following chord progression:

A 7th for 8 bars. (A Mixolydian mode.)
C 7th for 8 bars. (C Mixolydian mode.)
A 7th for 8 bars. (A Mixolydian mode.)

Make sure you change correctly from one Mixolydian mode to the other as indicated by the chord changes. Notice that there are four notes which appear in both the A Mixolydian and the C Mixolydian modes. They are: G, A, D, and E. Use these notes as pivot notes in your improvisation when changing from one mode to the other.

Exercise 4

This tune was composed by using the 1st, 3rd, 5th, 6th, and 7th, notes (degrees) in the D Mixolydian mode. After playing the melody, you should improvise by using all the notes in the mode.

The notes of the D Mixolydian mode are:

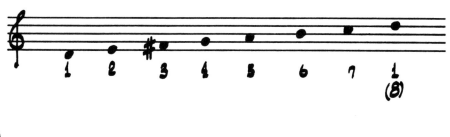

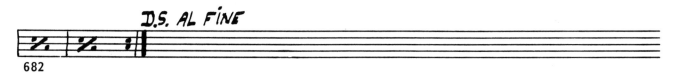

682

Exercise 5

This tune uses the 1st, 2nd, 5th and 6th notes (degrees) in the G Mixolydian mode. After playing the melody, try improvising by using all the notes in the mode.

The notes of the G Mixolydian mode are:

682

Exercise 6

This tune was composed combining Exercises 4 and 5. It is 24 bars long. Each chorus is constructed on the following chord progression:

D 7th for 8 bars. (D Mixolydian mode.)
G 7th for 8 bars. (G Mixolydian mode.)
D 7th for 8 bars. (D Mixolydian mode.)

As in exercise 3, make sure you change correctly from one Mixolydian mode to the other as indicated by the chord changes. Again, there are six notes held in common by both the D and the G Mixolydian modes. They are G, A, B, C, D, and E. These notes may be used as pivot notes for changing from one mode to the other, as you improvise.

682

23

Matteson Avenue

This tune is 16 bars long, and is based on two chords: A 7 and D 7. You will be using the A Mixolydian mode and the D Mixolydian mode. The six common tones between these modes are: A, B, D, E, F#, and G.

682

Bad Day At Jack Rock

This tune is 12 bars long. It is in rock style and based on three chords: A 7, C 7, and D 7. You will be using the A Mixolydian, C Mixolydian, and D Mixolydian modes. There are four notes which appear in all three of these modes. They are: A, D, E, and G. Use those common tones as pivot notes when changing from one chord to another.

682

25

Twelve Bars of Greens

This tune is twelve bars long, followed by repeats. It is based on three chords: G 7, C 7 and D 7
You will be using the G Mixolydian, the C Mixolydian, and the D Mixolydian modes. There are five notes held in common among these three. They are: G, A, C, D, and E.

12 Bars of Greens (Slow Version)

When playing this version, do not take the first ending after letter F. Take the second ending and D.S. al Fine.

26

Cycle Song

'Cycle Song' is eight measures long, and then repeats. It is based on four chords, with chord changes every two measures. The four chords are: A 7, D 7, G 7, and C 7. You will use the A Mixolydian mode, the D Mixolydian mode, the G Mixolydian mode and the C Mixolydian mode.

There are four notes that appear in all of these modes. These are: A, D, E and G. You will find still more common tones appearing between the chords as you play this tune. For example, there are six common tones in the A and D Mixolydian modes. There are also six common tones in the D and G Mixolydian modes. There are six common tones in G and C Mixolydian modes, and four in the C and the A Mixolydian modes. See if you can find them, and use them to create musical patterns that will fit both chords. When you listen to the soloists on the record, you will hear them do this. You will also hear them playing notes that are outside the mode. These are passing tones, and they may be used, but only with care. If you play a note that is not in the Mixolydian mode of a chord, you should then resolve that note by moving into a note that *is* in the mode. For example, if you are improvising to a G 7, using the G Mixolydian mode, and you play an A-flat, you should then play a note, such as an A-natural or a G, that is in the G Mixolydian mode. These "non-chordal" notes will add much to your melodic motion, as they help to build and release tension. However, do not use them in a careless manner, or your improvising will sound unorganized. Creating a good jazz solo is like creating a good recipe: Don't use more sugar than necessary, but don't use too much vinegar, either!!!

682

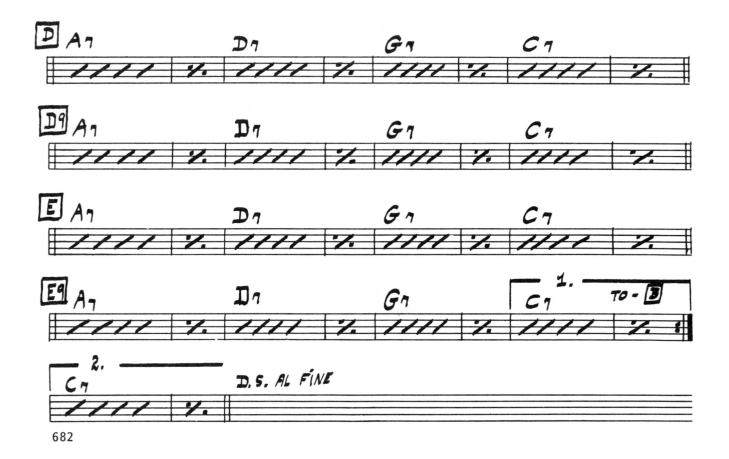

682

After working with Volume I and Volume II, you will find that Volumes III and IV are the next logical steps for you to take in your approach to jazz improvisational studies. Practice seriously and diligently, and we wish you pleasure and good luck!

—Rich Matteson

This record is Volume II in a series of MMO lp's designed to help teachers and students develop improvisational techniques. It is suggested that the student study Volume I before progressing to Volume II.

The entire volume is based on the Mixolydian mode; all chords used are dominant 7th chords. Because each chord must be treated as a V 7 chord comprising the first, third, fifth and seventh degrees of the Mixolydian mode, each will use its own Mixolydian scale.

The charts below will help you understand the Mixolydian mode and how it can be used with the dominant 7th (V 7) chord.

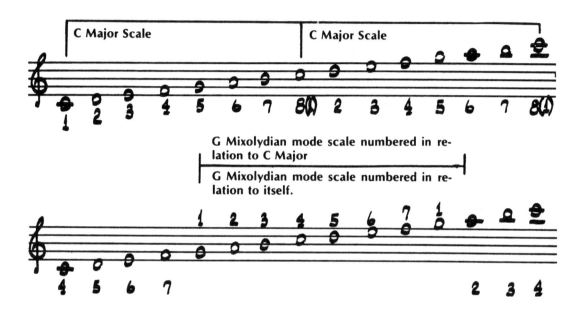

All the notes listed above are numbered to show their relationship to C Major.

All the notes below are numbered to show their relationship to G Mixolydian mode.

29

TUNING GUIDE

Instruments in E♭

Exercise I

This tune was composed using the 1st, 2nd, 3rd, and 4th notes (degrees) of the E Mixolydian mode. After playing the melody, you should improvise by using all the notes in the mode. (At this stage of your development, do not use any other notes.)

The notes of the E Mixolydian mode are:

682

Exercise 2

This tune uses only the 1st, 5th, and 7th notes (degrees) of the G Mixolydian mode. After playing the melody, you should improvise by using all of the notes in the mode.

The notes of the G Mixolydian mode are:

Exercise 3

This tune was composed by putting Exercises 1 and 2 together. It is 24 bars long. Each chorus is constructed by the following chord progression:

E 7th for 8 bars. (E Mixolydian mode.)
G 7th for 8 bars. (G Mixolydian mode.)
E 7th for 8 bars. (E Mixolydian mode.)

Make sure you change correctly from one Mixolydian mode to the other as indicated by the chord changes. Notice that there are four notes which appear in both the E Mixolydian and the G Mixolydian modes. They are: A, B, D, and E. Use these notes as pivot notes in your improvisation when changing from one mode to the other.

682

32

Exercise 4

This tune was composed by using the 1st, 3rd, 5th, 6th, and 7th notes (degrees) in the A Mixolydian mode. After playing the melody, you should improvise by using all the notes in the mode.

The notes of the A Mixolydian mode are:

682

33

Exercise 5

This tune uses the 1st, 2nd, 5th and 6th notes (degrees) in the D Mixolydian mode. After playing the melody, try improvising, using all the notes in the mode.

The notes of the D Mixolydian mode are:

Exercise 6

This tune was composed combining Exercises 4 and 5 together. It is 24 bars long. Each chorus is constructed on the following chord progression:

A 7th for 8 bars. (A Mixolydian mode.)
D 7th for 8 bars. (D Mixolydian mode.)
A 7th for 8 bars. (A Mixolydian mode.)

As in exercise 3, make sure you change correctly from one Mixolydian mode to the other as indicated by the chord changes. Again, there are six notes held in common by both the A and the D Mixolydian modes. They are D, E, F#, G, A, and B. These notes may be used as pivot notes for changing from one mode to the other, as you improvise.

D.S. AL FINE

682

Matteson Avenue

This tune is 16 bars long, and is based on two chords: E 7 and A 7. You will be using the E Mixolydian mode and the A Mixolydian mode. The six common tones between these modes are: E, F#, A, B, C#, and D.

Bad Day At Jack Rock

This tune is 12 bars long. It is in rock style and based on three chords: E 7, G 7, and A 7. You will be using the E Mixolydian, G Mixolydian, and A Mixolydian modes. There are four notes which appear in all three of these modes. They are: A, B, D, and E. Use those common tones as pivot notes when changing from one chord to another.

Twelve Bars of Greens

This tune is twelve bars long, followed by repeats. It is based on three chords: D 7, G 7, A 7. You will be using the D Mixolydian, the G Mixolydian, and the A Mixolydian modes. There are five notes held in common among these three. They are: D, E, G, A, and B.

12 Bars of Greens (Slow Version)

When playing this version, do not take the first ending after letter F. Take the second ending and D.S. al Fine.

Cycle Song

'Cycle Song' is eight measures long, and then repeats. It is based on four chords, with chord changes every two measures. The four chords are: E 7, A 7, D 7, and G 7. You will use the E Mixolydian mode, the A Mixolydian mode, the D Mixolydian mode and the G Mixolydian mode.

There are four notes that appear in all of these modes. These are: E, A, B, D. You will find still more common tones appearing between the chords as you play this tune. For example, there are six common tones in the E and A Mixolydian modes. There are also six common tones in the A and D Mixolydian modes. There are six common tones in D and G Mixolydian modes, and four in the G and E Mixolydian modes. See if you can find them, and use them to create musical patterns that will fit both chords. When you listen to the soloists on the record, you will hear them do this. You will also hear them playing notes that are outside the mode. These are passing tones, and they may be used, but only with care. If you play a note that is not in the Mixolydian mode of a chord, you should then resolve that note by moving into a note that *is* in the mode. For example, if you are improvising to a G 7, using the G Mixolydian mode, and you play an A-flat, you should then play a note, such as an A-natural or a G, that is in the G Mixolydian mode.

These "non-chordal" notes will add much to your melodic motion, as they help to build and release tension. However, do not use them in a careless manner, or your improvising will sound unorganized. Creating a good jazz solo is like creating a good recipe: Don't use more sugar than necessary, but don't use too much vinegar, either!!!

682

39

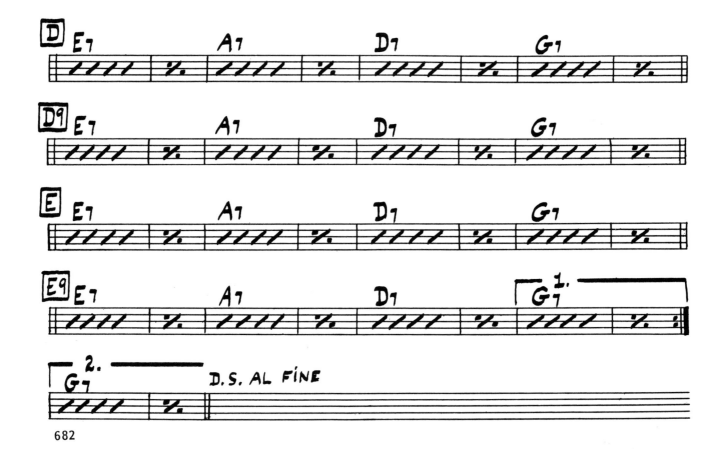

After working with Volume I and Volume II, you will find that Volumes III and IV are the next logical steps for you to take in your approach to jazz improvisational studies. Practice seriously and diligently, and we wish you pleasure and good luck!

—Rich Matteson

This record is Volume II in a series of MMO lp's designed to help teachers and students develop improvisational techniques. It is suggested that the student study Volume I before progressing to Volume II.

The entire volume is based on the Mixolydian mode; all chords used are dominant 7th chords. Because each chord must be treated as a V 7 chord comprising the first, third, fifth and seventh degrees of the Mixolydian mode, each will use its own Mixolydian scale.

The charts below will help you understand the Mixolydian mode and how it can be used with the dominant 7th (V 7) chord.

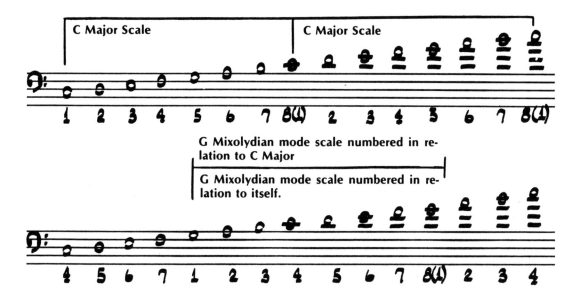

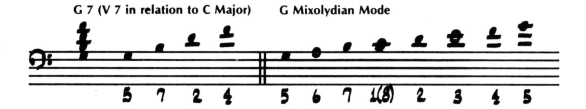

All the notes listed above are numbered to show their relationship to C Major.

All the notes below are numbered to show their relationship to G Mixolydian mode.

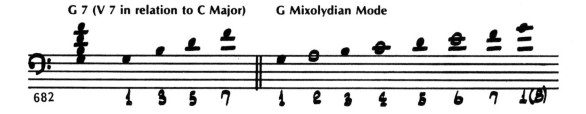

682

41

TUNING GUIDE

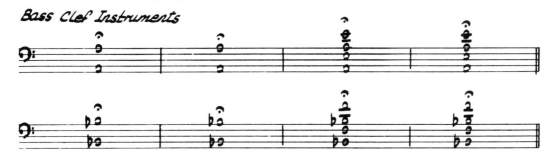

Bass Clef Instruments

Exercise I

This tune was composed using the 1st, 2nd, 3rd, and 4th notes (degrees) of the G Mixolydian mode. After playing the melody, you should improvise by using all the notes in the mode. (At this stage of your development, do not use any other notes.)

The notes of the G Mixolydian mode are:

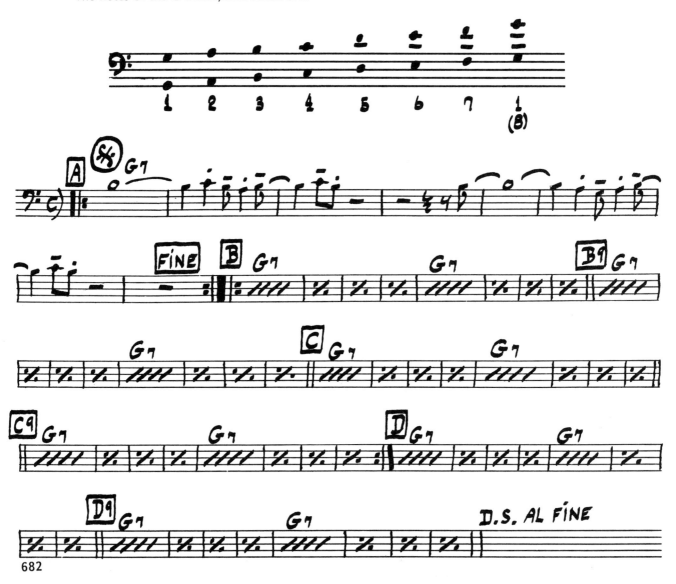

Exercise 2

This tune uses only the 1st, 5th, and 7th notes (degrees) of the Bb Mixolydian mode. After playing the melody, improvise using all of the notes in the mode.

The notes of the Bb Mixolydian mode are:

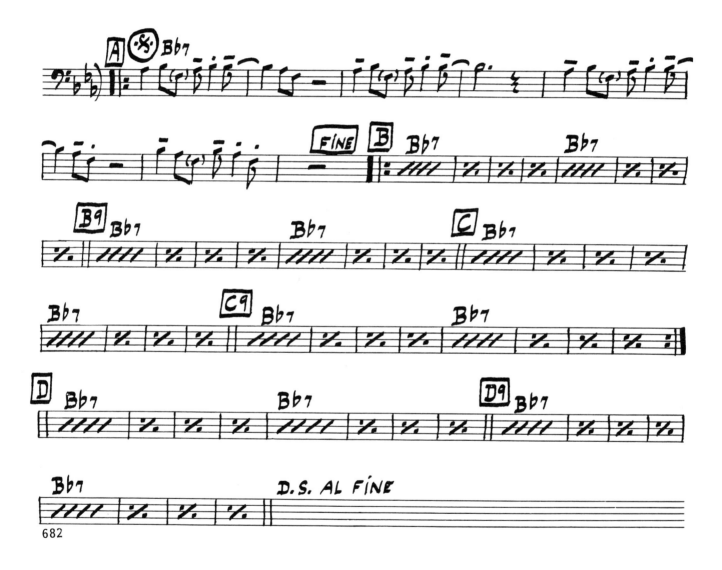

Exercise 3

This tune was composed by putting Exercises 1 and 2 together. It is 24 bars long. Each chorus is constructed by the following chord progression:

G 7th for 8 bars. (G Mixolydian mode.)
Bb 7th for 8 bars. (Bb Mixolydian mode.)
G 7th for 8 bars. (G Mixolydian mode.)

Make sure you change correctly from one Mixolydian mode to the other as indicated by the chord changes. Notice that there are four notes which appear in both the G Mixolydian and the Bb Mixolydian modes. They are: G, C, D, and F. Use these notes as pivot notes in your improvisation when changing from one mode to the other.

682

Exercise 4

This tune was composed by using the 1st, 3rd, 5th, 6th, and 7th, notes (degrees) in the C Mixolydian mode. After playing the melody, you should improvise by using all the notes in the mode.

The notes of the C Mixolydian mode are:

682

45

Exercise 5

This tune uses the 1st, 2nd, 5th and 6th notes (degrees) in the F Mixolydian mode. After playing the melody, try improvising, using all the notes in the mode.

The notes of the F Mixolydian mode are:

Exercise 6

This tune was composed combining Exercises 4 and 5. It is 24 bars long. Each chorus is constructed on the following chord progression:

C 7th for 8 bars. (C Mixolydian mode.)
F 7th for 8 bars. (F Mixolydian mode.)
C 7th for 8 bars. (C Mixolydian mode.)

As in exercise 3, make sure you change correctly from one Mixolydian mode to the other as indicated by the chord changes. Again, there are six notes held in common by both the C and the F Mixolydian modes. They are C, D, F, G, A and Bb. These notes may be used as pivot notes for changing from one mode to the other, as you improvise.

682

47

Matteson Avenue

This tune is 16 bars long, and is based on two chords: G7 and C7. You will be using the G Mixolydian mode and the C Mixolydian mode. The six common tones between these modes are: G, A, C, D, E, and F.

682

Bad Day At Jack Rock

This tune is 12 bars long. It is in rock style and based on three chords: G 7, Bb 7, and C 7. You will be using the G Mixolydian, Bb Mixolydian, and C Mixolydian, modes. There are four notes which appear in all three of these modes. They are: G, C, D, And F. Use those common tones as pivot notes when changing from one chord to another.

682

49

Twelve Bars of Greens

This tune is twelve bars long, followed by repeats. It is based on three chords: F 7, Bb 7, C 7. You will be using the F Mixolydian, the Bb Mixolydian, and the C Mixolydian, modes. There are five notes held in common among these three. They are: F, G, Bb, C, and D.

12 Bars of Greens (Slow Version)

When playing this version, do not take the first ending after letter F. Take the second ending and D.S. al Fine.

50

Cycle Song

'Cycle Song' is eight measures long, and then repeats. It is based on four chords, with chord changes every two measures. The four chords are: G 7, C 7, F 7, and Bb 7. You will use the G Mixolydian mode, the C Mixolydian mode, the F Mixolydian mode and the Bb Mixolydian mode. There are four notes that appear in all of these modes. These are: G, C, D, and F. You will find still more common tones appearing between the chords as you play this tune. For example,

There are six common tones in the G and C Mixolydian modes. There are also six common tones in the C and F Mixolydian modes. There are six common tones in the F and Bb Mixolydian modes, and four in the Bb and G Mixolydian modes. See if you can find them, and use them to create musical patterns that will fit both chords. When you listen to the soloists on the record, you will hear them do this. You will also hear them playing notes that are outside the mode.

These are passing tones, and they may be used, but only with care. If you play a note that is not in the Mixolydian mode of a chord, you should then resolve that note by moving into a note that *is* in the mode. For example, if you are improvising to a G 7, using the G Mixolydian mode, and you play an A-flat, you should then play a note, such as an A-natural or a G, that is in the G Mixolydian mode. These "non-chordal" notes will add much to your melodic motion, as they help to build and release tension. However, do not use them in a careless manner, or your improvising will sound unorganized. Creating a good jazz solo is like creating a good recipe: Don't use more sugar than necessary, but don't use too much vinegar, either!!!

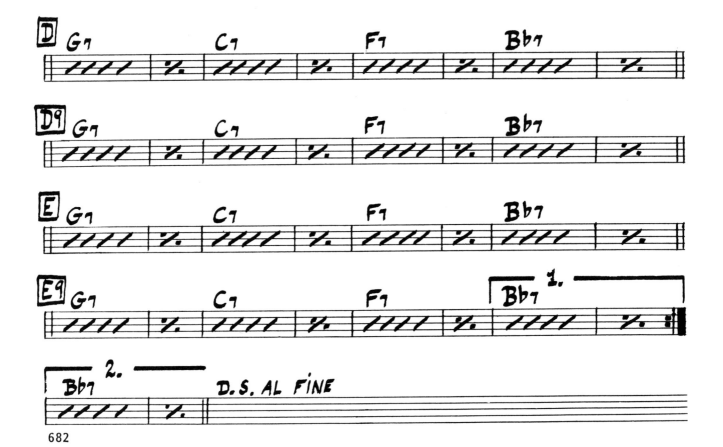

682

MMO Compact Disc Catalog

BROADWAY

LES MISERABLES/PHANTOM OF THE OPERA	MMO CD 1016
HITS OF ANDREW LLOYD WEBBER	MMO CD 1054
GUYS AND DOLLS	MMO CD 1067
WEST SIDE STORY 2 CD Set	MMO CD 1100
CABARET 2 CD Set	MMO CD 1110
BROADWAY HEROES AND HEROINES	MMO CD 1121
CAMELOT	MMO CD 1173
BEST OF ANDREW LLOYD WEBBER	MMO CD 1130
THE SOUND OF BROADWAY	MMO CD 1133
BROADWAY MELODIES	MMO CD 1134
BARBRA'S BROADWAY	MMO CD 1144
JEKYLL & HYDE	MMO CD 1151
SHOWBOAT	MMO CD 1160
MY FAIR LADY 2 CD Set	MMO CD 1174
OKLAHOMA	MMO CD 1175
THE SOUND OF MUSIC 2 CD Set	MMO CD 1176
SOUTH PACIFIC	MMO CD 1177
THE KING AND I	MMO CD 1178
FIDDLER ON THE ROOF 2 CD Set	MMO CD 1179
CAROUSEL	MMO CD 1180
PORGY AND BESS	MMO CD 1181
THE MUSIC MAN	MMO CD 1183
ANNIE GET YOUR GUN 2 CD Set	MMO CD 1186
HELLO DOLLY! 2 CD Set	MMO CD 1187
OLIVER 2 CD Set	MMO CD 1189
SUNSET BOULEVARD	MMO CD 1193
GREASE	MMO CD 1196
SMOKEY JOE'S CAFE	MMO CD 1197
MISS SAIGON	MMO CD 1226

CLARINET

MOZART CONCERTO, IN A, K.622	MMO CD 3201
WEBER CONCERTO NO. 1 in Fm. STAMITZ CONC. No. 3 IN Bb	MMO CD 3202
SPOHR CONCERTO NO. 1 in C MINOR OP. 26	MMO CD 3203
WEBER CONCERTO OP. 26, BEETHOVEN TRIO OP. 11	MMO CD 3204
FIRST CHAIR CLARINET SOLOS	MMO CD 3205
THE ART OF THE SOLO CLARINET:	MMO CD 3206
MOZART QUINTET IN A, K.581	MMO CD 3207
BRAHMS SONATAS OP. 120 NO. 1 & 2	MMO CD 3208
WEBER GRAND DUO CONCERTANT WAGNER ADAGIO	MMO CD 3209
SCHUMANN FANTASY OP. 73, 3 ROMANCES OP. 94	MMO CD 3210
EASY CLARINET SOLOS Volume 1 - STUDENT LEVEL	MMO CD 3211
EASY CLARINET SOLOS Volume 2 - STUDENT LEVEL	MMO CD 3212
EASY JAZZ DUETS - STUDENT LEVEL	MMO CD 3213
VISIONS The Clarinet Artistry of Ron Odrich	MMO CD 3214
IN A LEAGUE OF HIS OWN The Clarinet Artistry of Ron Odrich	MMO CD 3215
SINATRA SET TO MUSIC The Clarinet Artistry of Ron Odrich	MMO CD 3216
STRAVINSKY: L'HISTOIRE DU SOLDAT	MMO CD 3217
BEGINNING CONTEST SOLOS - Jerome Bunke, Clinician	MMO CD 3221
BEGINNING CONTEST SOLOS - Harold Wright	MMO CD 3222
INTERMEDIATE CONTEST SOLOS - Stanley Drucker	MMO CD 3223
INTERMEDIATE CONTEST SOLOS - Jerome Bunke, Clinician	MMO CD 3224
ADVANCED CONTEST SOLOS - Stanley Drucker	MMO CD 3225
ADVANCED CONTEST SOLOS - Harold Wright	MMO CD 3226
INTERMEDIATE CONTEST SOLOS - Stanley Drucker	MMO CD 3227
ADVANCED CONTEST SOLOS - Stanley Drucker	MMO CD 3228
ADVANCED CONTEST SOLOS - Harold Wright	MMO CD 3229
BRAHMS Clarinet Quintet in Bm, Op. 115	MMO CD 3230
TEACHER'S PARTNER Basic Clarinet Studies	MMO CD 3231
JEWELS FOR WOODWIND QUINTET	MMO CD 3232
WOODWIND QUINTETS minus CLARINET	MMO CD 3233
FROM DIXIE to SWING	MMO CD 3234
THE VIRTUOSO CLARINETIST Baermann Method, Op. 63 4 CD Set	MMO CD 3240
ART OF THE CLARINET. Baermann Method, Op. 64 4 CD Set	MMO CD 3241
POPULAR CONCERT FAVORITES WITH ORCHESTRA	MMO CD 3242
BAND-AIDS CONCERT BAND FAVORITES WITH ORCHESTRA	MMO CD 3243

PIANO

BEETHOVEN CONCERTO NO. 1 IN C	MMO CD 3001
BEETHOVEN CONCERTO NO. 2 IN Bb	MMO CD 3002
BEETHOVEN CONCERTO NO. 3 IN C MINOR	MMO CD 3003
BEETHOVEN CONCERTO NO. 4 IN G	MMO CD 3004
BEETHOVEN CONCERTO NO. 5 IN Eb (2 CD SET)	MMO CD 3005
GRIEG CONCERTO IN A MINOR OP.16	MMO CD 3006
RACHMANINOFF CONCERTO NO. 2 IN C MINOR	MMO CD 3007
SCHUMANN CONCERTO IN A MINOR	MMO CD 3008
BRAHMS CONCERTO NO. 1 IN D MINOR (2 CD SET)	MMO CD 3009
CHOPIN CONCERTO NO. 1 IN E MINOR OP. 11	MMO CD 3010

MENDELSSOHN CONCERTO NO. 1 IN G MINOR	MMO CD 3011
MOZART CONCERTO NO. 9 IN Eb K.271	MMO CD 3012
MOZART CONCERTO NO. 12 IN A K.414	MMO CD 3013
MOZART CONCERTO NO. 20 IN D MINOR K.466	MMO CD 3014
MOZART CONCERTO NO. 23 IN A K.488	MMO CD 3015
MOZART CONCERTO NO. 24 IN C MINOR K.491	MMO CD 3016
MOZART CONCERTO NO. 26 IN D K.537, CORONATION	MMO CD 3017
MOZART CONCERTO NO. 17 IN G K.453	MMO CD 3018
LISZT CONCERTO NO. 1 IN Eb, WEBER OP. 79	MMO CD 3019
LISZT CONCERTO NO. 2 IN A, HUNGARIAN FANTASIA	MMO CD 3020
J.S. BACH CONCERTO IN F MINOR, J.C. BACH CON. IN Eb	MMO CD 3021
J.S. BACH CONCERTO IN D MINOR	MMO CD 3022
HAYDN CONCERTO IN D	MMO CD 3023
HEART OF THE PIANO CONCERTO	MMO CD 3024
THEMES FROM GREAT PIANO CONCERTI	MMO CD 3025
TSCHAIKOVSKY CONCERTO NO. 1 IN Bb MINOR	MMO CD 3026
ART OF POPULAR PIANO PLAYING, Vol. 1 STUDENT LEVEL	MMO CD 3033
ART OF POPULAR PIANO PLAYING, Vol. 2 STUDENT LEVEL 2 CD Set	MMO CD 3034
'POP' PIANO FOR STARTERS STUDENT LEVEL	MMO CD 3035
DVORAK TRIO IN A MAJOR, OP. 90 "Dumky Trio"	MMO CD 3037
DVORAK QUINTET IN A MAJOR, OP. 81	MMO CD 3038
MENDELSSOHN TRIO IN D MAJOR, OP. 49	MMO CD 3039
MENDELSSOHN TRIO IN C MINOR, OP. 66	MMO CD 3040
BLUES FUSION FOR PIANO	MMO CD 3049
CLAUDE BOLLING SONATA FOR FLUTE AND JAZZ PIANO TRIO	MMO CD 3050
TWENTY DIXIELAND CLASSICS	MMO CD 3051
TWENTY RHYTHM BACKGROUNDS TO STANDARDS	MMO CD 3052
FROM DIXIE to SWING	MMO CD 3053
J.S. BACH BRANDENBURG CONCERTO NO. 5 IN D MAJOR	MMO CD 3054
BACH Cm CONC. - 2 PIANOS / SCHUMANN & VAR., OP. 46 - 2 PIANOS	MMO CD 3055
J.C. BACH Bm CONC./HAYDN C CONCERT./HANDEL CONC. GROSSO-D	MMO CD 3056
J.S. BACH TRIPLE CONCERTO IN A MINOR	MMO CD 3057
FRANCK SYM. VAR. / MENDELSSOHN: CAPRICCO BRILLANT	MMO CD 3058
C.P.E. BACH CONCERTO IN A MINOR	MMO CD 3059
STRETCHIN' OUT-'Comping' with a Jazz Rhythm Section	MMO CD 3060
RAVEL: PIANO TRIO	MMO CD 3061
GREAT STANDARDS FOR PIANO STUDENTS: Jim Odrich, piano	MMO CD 3062
MORE STANDARDS FOR PIANO STUDENTS: Jim Odrich, piano	MMO CD 3063
SCHUMANN: Piano Trio in D Minor, Opus 63	MMO CD 3064
BEETHOVEN: Trio No. 8 & Trio No. 11, "Kakadu" Variations	MMO CD 3065

PIANO - FOUR HANDS

RACHMANINOFF Six Scenes	4-5th year	MMO CD 3027
ARENSKY 6 Pieces, STRAVINSKY 3 Easy Dances	2-3rd year	MMO CD 3028
FAURE: The Dolly Suite		MMO CD 3029
DEBUSSY: Four Pieces		MMO CD 3030
SCHUMANN Pictures from the East	4-5th year	MMO CD 3031
BEETHOVEN Three Marches	4-5th year	MMO CD 3032
MOZART COMPLETE MUSIC FOR PIANO FOUR HANDS 2 CD Set		MMO CD 3036
MAYKAPAR First Steps, OP. 29	1-2nd year	MMO CD 3041
TSCHAIKOVSKY: 50 Russian Folk Songs		MMO CD 3042
BIZET: 12 Children's Games		MMO CD 3043
GRETCHANINOFF: ON THE GREEN MEADOW		MMO CD 3044
POZZOLI: SMILES OF CHILDHOOD		MMO CD 3045
DIABELLI: PLEASURES OF YOUTH		MMO CD 3046
SCHUBERT: FANTASIA & GRAND SONATA		MMO CD 3047

VIOLIN

BRUCH CONCERTO NO. 1 IN G MINOR OP.26	MMO CD 3100
MENDELSSOHN CONCERTO IN E MINOR	MMO CD 3101
TSCHAIKOVSKY CONCERTO IN D OP. 35	MMO CD 3102
BACH DOUBLE CONCERTO IN D MINOR	MMO CD 3103
BACH CONCERTO IN A MINOR, CONCERTO IN E	MMO CD 3104
BACH BRANDENBURG CONCERTI NOS. 4 & 5	MMO CD 3105
BACH BRANDENBURG CONCERTO NO. 2, TRIPLE CONCERTO	MMO CD 3106
BACH CONCERTO IN DM, (FROM CONCERTO FOR HARPSICHORD)	MMO CD 3107
BRAHMS CONCERTO IN D OP. 77	MMO CD 3108
CHAUSSON POEME, SCHUBERT RONDO	MMO CD 3109
LALO SYMPHONIE ESPAGNOLE	MMO CD 3110
MOZART CONCERTO IN D K.218, VIVALDI CON. AM OP.3 NO.6	MMO CD 3111
MOZART CONCERTO IN A K.219	MMO CD 3112
WIENIAWSKI CON. IN D. SARASATE ZIGEUNERWEISEN	MMO CD 3113
VIOTTI CONCERTO NO. 22 IN A MINOR	MMO CD 3114
BEETHOVEN 2 ROMANCES, SONATA NO. 5 IN F "SPRING SONATA"	MMO CD 3115
SAINT-SAENS INTRODUCTION & RONDO,	
MOZART SERENADE K. 204, ADAGIO K.261	MMO CD 3116
BEETHOVEN CONCERTO IN D OP. 61(2 CD SET)	MMO CD 3117
THE CONCERTMASTER - Orchestral Excerpts	MMO CD 3118
AIR ON A G STRING Favorite Encores with Orchestra Easy Medium	MMO CD 3119
CONCERT PIECES FOR THE SERIOUS VIOLINIST Easy Medium	MMO CD 3120
18TH CENTURY VIOLIN PIECES	MMO CD 3121

MMO Compact Disc Catalog

MMO Music Group • 50 Executive Boulevard, Elmsford, New York 10523, 1-(800) 669-7464
Website: www. minusone.com • E-mail: mmomus@aol.com

MMO Compact Disc Catalog

MMO Music Group • 50 Executive Boulevard, Elmsford, New York 10523, 1-(800) 669-7464
Website: www. minusone.com • E-mail: mmomus@aol.com